AMAZING ACHIEVEMENT DAYS

Jennifer Jackson and Beth Lefgren

Illustrated by Jeni Gochnour

Bookcraft
Salt Lake City, Utah

ISBN 1-57008-221-9
Library of Congress Catalog Card Number: 95-83306

First Printing, 1996

Printed in the United States of America

Contents

Arts and Crafts

Education and Scholarship

Family History

Family Skills

Health and Personal Grooming

Hospitality

Outdoor Fun and Skills

Personal Preparedness

Safety and Emergency Preparedness

Service and Citizenship

Spirituality

Sports and Physical Fitness

Preface

What a thrill it was to work on this book! Activities provide unlimited opportunities to strengthen and teach the young people around us. They can supply a great deal of fun in a gospel-oriented atmosphere. What better way to reach each child than through wholesome, enjoyable activities?

Even though this book was written and formatted for achievement days, we found that many of these activities work well for family home evening and Young Women/ Young Men activities. Your own personal creativity and knowledge of the age group can easily adapt most of these ideas to other programs.

In writing this book, we tried to stay away from time-consuming preparation and costly materials, allowing you to focus on the children in your stewardship. In addition, every activity in this book has been tried (and approved) by children.

We wish you well in whatever capacity you will be using this book. We know that you will find great blessings in working with these young brothers and sisters, and we hope that this book will assist you in achieving the best possible program.

How to Use This Book

This book contains a wide variety of activities. We have endeavored to offer a large selection to meet your specific needs. To assist in the use of these activities, the following suggestions may be helpful:

1. Notice that the activities are grouped into the twelve areas of achievement as outlined in the achievement days program. However, most activities can easily be adjusted to meet goals for Young Women, Young Men, or family home evenings.

2. Many activities can be interchanged into other achievement areas. For example, a "Service and Citizenship" activity of cooking a meal for someone else might easily be used to fulfill requirements in the "Family Skills" category. You will discover a greater variety and flexibility as you familiarize yourself with all the activities in this book.

3. Many of the activities have been cross-referenced for your convenience. For instance, an "Arts and Crafts" activity of making greeting cards is cross-referenced to a "Hospitality" activity on writing thank-you notes. The cross-references suggest additional activities that will strengthen and support your current goals.

4. Consider the specific needs of your group when planning your activities. The number of children, their ages, the amount of time, and your facilities are all important factors to success. These activities can easily be modified to fit your specific needs.

5. Parents and other adults in your ward are tremendous resources. Inquire about specific talents of these individuals and use them often! For example, if you know of someone who is a beautician, enlist his or her help in personal grooming activities. Always consider outside resources for help and expertise.

6. Family support will be a great help to your group. For this purpose, an achievement days calendar is offered in the back of the book. Regular use of this calendar will inform parents of the achievement goals their child is currently working on, as well as inform them of dates, times, and places. A sample calendar is also included to give you further details.

7. Most of the lessons have a "Family Ideas" section for follow-up. These follow-up activities will help to increase parental involvement in this wonderful program. In addition, they will enrich the children's experiences in each of the achievement areas. These ideas can also be listed on your family calendar.

8. To assist with your recognition meetings, we have included several recognition certificates in the back of this book. You may desire to present the children with a certificate as they successfully complete the goals of each achievement section.

We know that as you apply these guidelines you will experience wonderful success.

Arts and Crafts

*To help me learn about the creative arts
and develop my artistic talents.*

Making a Scripture Picture

Materials Needed

Heavy parchment paper and a small, inexpensive frame with a glass front for each child, pencils, rulers, scissors, fine-tipped permanent black markers, glue stick.

Before You Meet

Gather several small individual leaves (such as honey locust, small rose, etc.) and small flowers (such as dianthus, violet, lilac, etc.) It is not necessary to press these items before this achievement activity.

Activity

- Cut a piece of parchment slightly smaller than the frame (about 1/8 inch smaller on each side).
- Decide on a hymn title or short, favorite scripture.
- Draw faint lines in the middle of the parchment and carefully write the hymn title or scripture in pencil above the lines. Carefully trace the writing with the permanent marker. Erase any pencil marks.
- Lay the parchment on top of the frame's cardboard backing.
- Place the single petals and small leaves in a pattern around the written part. Secure by using a tiny amount of glue from the glue stick.
- Clean and thoroughly dry the glass and lay it on the parchment. Be careful not to disturb the petal/leaf pattern.
- Carefully place the glass, parchment, and cardboard backing into the frame and secure.

Family Ideas

Help your child find a place where the picture can be seen.

Making a Drawstring Bag

Materials Needed

Two sewing machines, thread, straight pins, safety pins, scissors, yarn.

Before You Meet

Depending on the size of your group, you may want to arrange for an additional assistant. Ask children to bring a piece of scrap fabric, cut in a 10" x 20" rectangle. You may follow up this activity with "Making a Stencil" on p. 6 to decorate your bags.

Activity

- Fold fabric in half with right sides together. Pin the sides and sew with a straight stitch. Use a 1/2- to 5/8-inch seam allowance. This should form a bag with the opening at the top and the fold at the bottom.
- Fold down one inch of fabric at the top of the bag, wrong sides together. Sew 1/2 inch from the edge of the fabric around the top of the bag, leaving a one-inch opening for the drawstring.
- Cut three pieces of yarn twenty-five inches long. Tie all three together with a knot at one end. Braid the yarn, and knot the other end.
- Put a safety pin in one of the knots. Use this to help feed the yarn through the casing at the top of the bag. Remove the safety pin, and turn the bag right side out.
- Discuss ideas for uses of the drawstring bags.

Family Ideas

Use scrap fabric to make additional bags for game pieces, marbles, blocks, cookie cutters, and much more.

Rhythm Instruments and Fun Songs

Materials Needed

Empty one-liter bottle, one-half cup rice or macaroni, two metal spoons, twelve-inch piece of twine, cookie sheet, four or five large rubber bands, loose buttons of assorted sizes, two disposable aluminum pie plates, stapler.

Before You Meet

Decide on a project or performance in which you can use the songs and rhythm instruments.

Activity

- Make the following rhythm makers or use other ideas.

  Foil tambourine: Place fifteen to twenty buttons in one pie plate. Cover with the other pie plate. Staple or tape the edges shut. Shake or tap to the rhythm.
  Cookie sheet guitar: Place large rubber bands around a cookie sheet. Strum like a guitar.
  Spoon chime: Tie one spoon at the end of the twine and allow to hang. Gently strike the hanging spoon with a second spoon.
  Rattle: Place one-half cup of rice or macaroni inside an empty one-liter bottle. Close tightly. Shake using both hands.

- Practice using the rhythm instruments as you sing fun songs. Choose from the following ideas or use some of your own.

  "She'll Be Comin' Round the Mountain": Substitute the rhythm sounds for spoken words. (Example: "She'll be comin' round the mountain when she comes," *chime, chime.*)
  "Bingo": Replace the missing letter with a rhythm sound. (Example: *shake, rattle,* "N," "G," "O.")
  "If You're Happy and You Know It": Use rhythm sounds as you "clap your hands," "stomp your feet," etc.

- Decide which song(s) you want to perform.

Family Ideas

Encourage your child to have fun as she sings and performs. If possible, plan to be at the project/performance for support.

Making a Stencil

Materials Needed

Heavy paper (file folders work well), sharp-pointed scissors, several coloring books with simple designs, pencils, a stencil paintbrush, paint (available at craft and variety stores).

Before You Meet

Make your own stencil for a demonstration during the activity. Sort through the coloring books to find simple designs and pictures that could be made into an easy stencil. You may follow up this activity with "Making a Drawstring Bag" on p. 4, using the stencil to decorate the bags.

Activity

- Let the children look through the coloring books to find an easy picture or shape they would like a stencil of.
- Have the children cut their pictures out.
- Trace around each picture onto the heavy paper.
- Cut out the inside of each picture, leaving the frame around it intact.
- Demonstrate how to use a stencil by placing it on a piece of paper and coloring or painting in the cut-out section.

Family Ideas

Help your child find a special place to use the stencil: a tote bag, a pillowcase, a T-shirt, and so on.

Children's Theater

Materials Needed

Paper, pencils, costume and stage equipment.

Before You Meet

This activity may be divided into four meetings: planning, costumes and settings, practice, and performance. Each meeting can fulfill different achievement requirements. For example, preparation of the costumes and set could be used as an arts and crafts project, while the performance could be done at a nursing home as a service project.

Gather a few script ideas. Short children's stories, historical events, and scripture stories work well.

Activity

- Prepare a simple script. Use a narrator to help with transitions.
- Assign all parts.
- Schedule a performance date and place.
- Plan and prepare simple costumes and props.
- Practice.
- Perform. (Consider nursing homes, parents, ward gatherings, and Primary activities.)

Family Ideas

Encourage your child to fulfill her assignment for the performance. Invite the family to see the production.

Making Greeting Cards

Materials Needed

Two pieces (8 1/2" x 11") of good quality paper for each child, tempera or acrylic paint, black permanent markers, cut sponges, rulers, pencils.

Before You Meet

Cut a sponge into small cubes (about one inch in size). Do this activity yourself to acquaint yourself with how it is done.

Activity

- Have the children decide what kind of greeting cards they want to make.
- Give each child two pieces of paper.
- Measure with the ruler and use the pencil to divide the paper into three equal pieces.
- Turn the paper over and use the damp (not wet) sponges to dot the paper with paint.
- After the paint has dried, cut the paper on the measuring lines and fold each note in half.
- On the front of each note write or print the appropriate words (*thanks, congratulations, happy birthday, get well,* etc.).
- Encourage the children to use them for friends and family.

Making Puppets

Materials Needed

Materials are dependent upon the type of puppet and puppet theater you decide to use. You may decide to use more than one kind of puppet.

Before You Meet

Decide on a simple story or fairy tale to use with your puppets. Plan a project or performance in which you can use the puppets.

Activity

- Use one of the following ideas to develop your puppets or use some of your own.

    Stick puppet: Draw and color a figure on a piece of heavy paper or cardboard. Cut the figure out and glue to a tongue depressor or Popsicle stick.

    Finger puppet: Draw a two- to three-inch figure without legs on a piece of heavy paper. Color. Cut holes to allow your first two fingers to be the "legs" of the puppet. Paint the fingers the color of pants, dress, etc. Be sure to use the kind of paint that washes off.

    Stuffed sack puppet: Open a small paper sack and stuff with newspaper. Tie the stuffed "head" to a small stick. Draw or glue features for the face. Make the costume by using a large square of construction paper or material. Cut a hole in the center and insert the stuffed head through it. Tie or glue the costume to the bottom of the head and fold it down to cover the stick.

    Paper plate puppet: Staple two paper plates together. Leave a gap at the bottom large enough to get your hand through. Use scraps of material, paper, markers, or crayons to make a face. Be sure that the gap is at the bottom of the face.

- Make one of the following puppet theaters. Keep in mind the size and kind of puppets you will be using.

    Table stage: Turn a table on its side and kneel behind it. Hold puppets over the edge of the table.

    Doorway stage: Secure a sheet to cover the bottom two-thirds of the doorway. Perform above the sheet. If possible, keep the room behind the performance area dark.

    Cardboard table stage: Cut a square from one side of a large cardboard box. Keep in mind that this will be the stage or performing area. Decorate the rest of the cardboard box with bright colored paints or markers. Drape a cloth around three sides of a table. Place the box on the table. Sit or kneel behind the table as the puppets perform on the stage.

- Practice the story or fairy tale with new puppets.

Family Ideas

Ask your child to help you make puppets for a family home evening.

Making a Leather-Look Vase

Materials Needed

Masking tape, paste shoe polish, polyurethane spray, paper towels (or a rag) for each child, newspaper.

Before You Meet

Ask each child to bring an old bottle or vase.

Activity

- Spread newspaper on the working area.
- Give each child some masking tape to tear into small, uneven pieces. As they tear the tape, have them put it on their bottle or vase. Repeat until the entire vase is covered with masking tape. Some overlapping is necessary.
- Cover the masking tape with paste shoe polish and then carefully wipe off the excess with a rag.
- Spray the finished project with polyurethane spray.
- Have the children assist in cleanup. Encourage them to use the vases, or plan on giving them as part of a gift.

Education and Scholarship

To encourage me to succeed in school
and set goals for my education.

Having an Education Fair

Materials Needed

Check selected sections for materials needed.

Before You Meet

Involve other adults in the setup and application of this program. Make signs for each area.

Activity

- Discuss with the children the many fields in education and scholarship. Help them understand that sometimes an area of study is called by a scientific name but the ideas that can be learned are exciting.
- Direct the children to the exhibits. Use two or more of the following, or others of your own choosing.

  Astronomy: Have the children look through a "stargazer." Make a stargazer by using an empty cardboard tube from paper towels. Cut a circle of black paper one inch larger than the tube. Use tape or a rubber band to secure the black paper over one end of the tube. Punch or prick holes in the shape of a constellation. Use a different stargazer for each constellation.

  Biology: Set up a microscope with slides of plant cells and animal cells. Have the children look into the microscope. This is an excellent time to teach them how to look through a microscope correctly.

  Geology: Show a rock collection. Have someone knowledgeable tell about the different rocks and where they are found.

  Magnetism: Use a magnet and several assorted items. Have the children choose which items will be picked up by the magnet.

  History: Have several historic happenings written on paper and have the children arrange them in the correct chronological order. Some ideas might include: pioneers come west, Columbus discovers America, astronauts land on the moon, Greeks hold the first Olympics, etc.

- Have a closing ceremony.

Family Ideas

Talk with your child about what she has learned.

A Visit with a Teacher

Materials Needed

Thank-you card, envelope, stamp, pen.

Before You Meet

Call a local school. Ask the principal to recommend a teacher who could discuss good study habits with your group. (Avoid using teachers that the children currently have.)

Contact the teacher and schedule a date and time. Ask the teacher to meet with the children in the classroom and teach them about good study habits and their importance.

Provide for adequate transportation, if necessary. Fill out any travel permits required by your ward or stake.

Activity

- Introduce the teacher to the children.
- Invite the teacher to make the presentation on good study habits.
- Follow up by letting children sign and mail a thank-you note to the teacher.

Family Ideas

Ask your child to share with the family what she learned.

Making a Book Cover

Materials Needed

Plain paper, such as butcher paper or paper sacks, for every child; markers for decoration, if desired.

Before You Meet

Have each child bring a book that she would like to make a cover for. (Hardcover books work best for this beginning activity.)

Activity

- Lay the book out flat, cover down, and measure its dimensions.
- Cut a piece of paper three inches larger than the book dimensions.
- If you desire, decorate one side of the plain paper with magic markers.
- Fold the top and bottom of the paper about 1 1/2 inches down (toward center). The cover should be the same height as the book.
- Fold the right side in toward the center.
- Place the book's cover inside the right side fold.
- Fold the left side to match the size of the book and slip the left book cover inside the fold.

Family Ideas

Talk with your child about why it is important to care for books correctly. This may be a good time to discuss how you feel about books and literacy.

Using the Library

Before You Meet

Call the librarian to schedule your visit to the library. Request a tour and an explanation of how to locate books and other resources in the library.

Provide for adequate transportation, if necessary. Fill out any travel permits required by your ward or stake.

Activity

- Tour the library.
- Teach the children how to locate books and other materials in the library.
- Assign each child a topic such as gardening, skiing, dancing, poetry, and so on. Tell them to locate a book or other resource about their topic using the instructions they were just given. Help them as needed.

Family Ideas

Get a library card if needed, and allow your child to check out a book.

A Book Review

Materials Needed

A list of book review questions for each child, refreshments.

Before You Meet

Notify the children and their parents that they need to read a book before the next meeting. Request them to tell the group about it at the activity. Give the children a list of the following questions to help them prepare their book review.

1. What type of book was it? (fiction/nonfiction)
2. What was the book about?
3. What did you like best about the book?
4. What did you dislike about the book?
5. What did you learn by reading this book?
6. Would you recommend this book to others? Why or why not?

Read a book and prepare to review it.
Plan and prepare refreshments.

Activity

- Serve refreshments, allowing the children to eat during the book review.
- Let everyone in the group take a turn telling about the book she read. Note: If any of the children did not read a book, encourage them to tell about a book they have previously read.

Family Ideas

Choose a book that the entire family would enjoy. Take a few minutes each day to read it together.

Read-a-Thon

Materials Needed

Books, pillows, and refreshments for everyone. (You may want to bring a few extra.)

Before You Meet

Assign each child to bring an enjoyable book, a pillow, and a refreshment to share with the group.

Activity

- Arrange all the refreshments on a table.
- Explain to the group that they should find a comfortable place to read their book and enjoy the refreshments. Remind them that no talking is allowed and that they must get the refreshments quietly so they don't disturb others.
- Quiet reading and refreshments.

Family Ideas

Plan a family reading night.

Making Flash Cards

Materials Needed

Index cards (or heavy paper cut to the appropriate size), marking pens.

Before You Meet

Determine how many cards you will need for each child to make a set of addition, subtraction, multiplication, or division flash cards. Consider the age and ability of your group as you decide which sets to do.

Activity

- Give each child a set of cards and a marking pen. Instruct them to write the math equation on one side and the answer on the back. Begin with equations that have the answer zero, and progress through those with the answer ten.
- Divide into pairs and practice using the flash cards. Challenge the children to practice often.

Family Ideas

Help your child use the flash cards to practice math problems. More cards can be made at home to help the child master addition, subtraction, multiplication, and division problems.

Family History

*To help me learn about my family
and how we can be together forever.*

Making Scrapbooks

Materials Needed

Tabbed notebook divider sheets (three for each child), clear plastic photograph display sheets (one for each child), clear plastic sheet protectors (two for each child).

Before You Meet

Ask the children to bring the following: an inexpensive three-ring binder, two or three personal or family photographs, one or two school papers or drawings, one or two personal award or recognition certificates.

Activity

- Label the tab dividers as follows: Schoolwork, Photographs, and Awards. Place in binders.
- Insert schoolwork back to back in a plastic sheet protector. Place it in the "Schoolwork" section.
- Label backs of photographs and insert into photograph display sheets. Place it in the "Photograph" section.
- Insert award certificates back to back in a plastic sheet protector. Place it in the "Awards" section.
- Encourage the children to continue adding to their scrapbooks.

Family Ideas

Look at family photos with your child. Label and organize your family's pictures.

Learning to Keep a Personal Journal

Materials Needed

A small, inexpensive folder and paper for each child, markers, stickers (or use the stencil from "Making a Stencil," p. 6).

Before You Meet

Copy the "Journal Thoughts and Ideas" page (see p. 25) for each child and place in the front of each folder.

Activity

- Talk with the children about what a journal is.
- If you have access to one, read some excerpts from a journal.
- Give every child a journal folder.
- Look at the "Journal Thoughts and Ideas" page and talk about some of the things that could go in a journal. Tell them to write about new things every day.
- Ask the children to date and make their first journal entry. Encourage them to use an idea from the list.
- Have them personalize and decorate the front of their journals.
- Encourage them to write regularly.

Family Ideas

Set aside some time once a week to write family events in a family journal.

Journal Thoughts and Ideas

Achievements

Advice

Baby blessings

Baptism

Blessings from Heavenly Father

Daily activities and surroundings

Family activities

Family home evenings

Family reunions

Genealogy

Goals

Happy experiences

Ideas from lessons

Missionary farewells and homecomings

People I have met

Places I have seen

Priesthood blessings

Priesthood ordinations

Sacred experiences

Sad times

School experiences

Someone who has helped me

Special times and moments

Spiritual thoughts

Testimonies I hear

Things I have learned

Weather conditions

Sharing Family Traditions

Before You Meet

Contact the parents of each child and explain the purpose of this activity. Ask them to discuss some of their family traditions together and to decide on one they will share with the group. A tradition can be a song, story, activity, item, or recipe.

Activity

- Gather the children together and talk about what a tradition is. Discuss some traditions they might all be familiar with and how they might have begun. Explain why traditions are important to families.
- Invite each child and parent to share their tradition with the group.
- Thank everyone for sharing their family traditions.
- Ask one of the children to offer a closing prayer.

Family Ideas

Talk about traditions in your family, why they began, and who might have started them.

Learning to Conduct Family History Interviews

Materials Needed

Tape recorder, blank audio tape, paper and pencils for every child, stationery.

Before You Meet

Call an elderly member of your ward and ask if the children can interview him or her. Explain the purpose of this achievement day activity.

Make arrangements for transportation, if necessary.

Activity

- Gather the children and explain what an interviewer does.
- Discuss what kind of questions a family history interviewer would ask. Write the questions down.
- Give each child a piece of paper and a pencil. Encourage them to take notes.
- Tell the children that a good interviewer uses a tape recorder for a backup. Ask them to tell you why.
- Meet with the elderly ward member.
- Take out the tape recorder. Explain to the brother or sister why you are using the tape recorder.
- Have the children ask questions. Use other questions and statements to clarify or find additional information. Do not overstay your time!
- Have each child write the ideas they remember from the interview. Use good stationery for this part.
- Encourage them to do the same for their parents or grandparents.
- Give the children's written histories to the person you visited. He or she will cherish them.

Family Ideas

Find a time when you and your child can interview a grandparent or older aunt or uncle. Help your child write or type the interview. Place the finished story in your family history book (see "Family Journals," p. 28).

Family Journals

Materials Needed

An inexpensive notebook and pen for each child, two or three black markers.

Before You Meet

Ask the children to come prepared to share a special family experience with the group. Encourage them to discuss ideas with their families.

Activity

- Let each child take a turn sharing a special experience with the group.
- Pass out notebooks. Have the children use a marker to label their notebook "Family Journal." Also have them write their last name on the front.
- Pass out the pens. Instruct the children to write down the family experience that they just shared with the group. Remind them to include the date.
- Encourage the children to continue to record their special experiences in their family journal.

Family Ideas

Each week let a different family member record special family memories in the journal.

Family Skills

*To give me opportunities to help my
family now and in the future.*

Learning to Read Food Labels

Before You Meet

Ask each child to bring a can of fruit or vegetables, any kind. You may want to follow up this lesson with the "A Grocery Store Field Trip," p. 35.

Activity

- Gather the children around a table or in a circle on the floor.
- Using the label on your can, show where to find the net weight. Explain what *net weight* is. Ask each child to tell the kind of food they have in their can and what its net weight is.
- Repeat the above process using other general information on the can. Use information such as: first ingredient, serving size, servings per can, kind of vitamins it has, etc.
- Explain that this information is found on most food cans and boxes. Talk about the freshness dates found on dairy and other products. Discuss the importance of knowing how to find this information.
- If time permits, talk about how to tell if produce is fresh.

Family Ideas

Help your child remember what she has learned by having her explain what information she finds on labels at home.

Learning to Use a Recipe

Materials Needed

Ingredients for the recipe you intend to make as a group, enough index cards for each child to copy the four recipes, pencils.

Before You Meet

Select four basic recipes for your group to copy onto index cards to start their own recipe file. Choose one of these recipes to make with the children.

Activity

- Teach the group how to read a recipe. Remind them to always read the entire recipe before beginning and to check to make sure they have all the necessary ingredients.
- Prepare the selected recipe with the group. You may proceed to the next activity step during the baking time.
- Give the children index cards and pencils, and instruct them to copy the four recipes. If desired, discuss recipe files and the ways they can be organized.

Family Ideas

Give your child the opportunity to prepare another recipe for the family.

Learning About Basic Mending

Materials Needed

Large table or flat working surface, squares of fabric, buttons, needles, thread, scissors.

Activity

- Teach the children how to thread a needle.
- Teach them how to sew on a button.
- Teach them how to sew a basic hemming stitch.

Family Ideas

Gather all the clothes that need to be mended. Work together to get it all done.

Laundry Tips

Materials Needed

A variety of laundry items (various colors, fabrics, and clothing items), a timer, liquid soap, small pieces of fabric, jam.

Activity

- Teach the children how to read the garment care labels in clothing. Explain what *dry clean* means. Caution them to always read the labels when they do the laundry.
- Teach the children how to sort the laundry. Have a sorting race. Give them two tries to sort a pile of clothing; challenge them to beat their first time.
- Teach the children how to remove basic spots. Explain that the quicker you wash the spot off, the easier it will come out. You must remove stains and spots before washing them in the machine. Rub a small spot of jam onto a piece of old fabric. Demonstrate how you use cool water and liquid soap to rub the spot away. Give each child a chance to try this.
- Teach the children how to fold clothes. Demonstrate folding shirts, pants, and towels. Let the group practice folding. Stress neatness to avoid wrinkles.

Family Ideas

Teach your child how to use the washer and dryer, if she is of the appropriate age.

A Grocery Store Field Trip

Materials Needed

Thank-you note, envelope, stamp, pen.

Before You Meet

Notify the manager of a local grocery store or market. Many times managers will be willing to provide you with a tour of their departments. If not, ask if you can do so on your own.

Provide for adequate transportation, if necessary. Fill out any travel permits required by your ward or stake.

You may wish to use this activity as a follow-up for the "Learning to Read Food Labels" activity, p. 31.

Activity

- Gather the children together and briefly talk about what you will see and do. Take this time to establish basic rules for this activity.
- Go to the store. If there is no tour provided, talk with the children about what happens in the different parts of the store, what might make this store different from others, the variety of brands that might be available, and so on.
- Have the children write and sign a thank-you note.

A Baby-Sitting Workshop

Materials Needed

Supplies as requested by teachers, refreshments.

Before You Meet

Arrange for the mothers of four of the children in your group to teach the following workshop sections: "Keeping Children Safe," "Making a Simple Toy," "Easy Snacks for Children," and "Fun and Games." You may want to follow up this activity with "Helping in the Nursery" on p. 86.

Activity

- Welcome and introduce the teachers.
- Rotate children to the four different workshop sections.
- Serve refreshments.

Family Ideas

Make a baby-sitting kit with fun games, toys, books, and so on. When members of the family go baby-sitting they can take the kit with them.

Health and Personal Grooming

To help me keep the Word of Wisdom and be an example of Latter-day Saint cleanliness, grooming, and modesty.

A Visit to the Dentist

Materials Needed

Thank-you card, envelope, stamp, pen.

Before You Meet

Schedule a date and time for the group to tour a dentist's office. Ask for the dentist or hygenist to take a few minutes and discuss good dental care with the children. Request an informative pamphlet that they can take home.

Provide for adequate transportation, if necessary. Fill out any travel permits required by your ward or stake.

Activity

- Tour the dentist's office.
- Have the presentation on good dental care.
- Let your group sign and mail a thank-you card following the activity.

Family Ideas

Review the dental care pamphlet as a family.

A Hospital Field Trip

Materials Needed

Thank-you note, envelope, stamp, pen.

Before You Meet

Contact the public relations department at a local hospital about the field trip. Explain that the objective of the field trip is to help acquaint the children with the purposes of a hospital. Make arrangements for a guide.

Provide for adequate transportation, if necessary. Fill out any travel permits required by your ward or stake.

Activity

- Take the children to the hospital.
- Be prepared to assist where needed.
- After returning from the hospital, write and send a thank-you note.

Family Ideas

Be prepared to discuss your child's feelings about the hospital.

Personal Cleanliness

Materials Needed

Washcloth, bar of soap, nail clippers, brush, comb, toothbrush, toothpaste, floss, old magazines, piece of poster board for each child.

Activity

- Show the different personal care items to the children.
- Talk about how cleanliness is a good defense against disease.
- Briefly discuss how these items are used to keep your body clean and healthy.

> *Bathing:* Use soap as you wash your body on a daily basis. When you can't get a full bath or shower, you can use a wet washcloth or towel. Show how this is done.
>
> *Hair:* Wash your hair often enough to keep it free of dirt and oil. Brush your hair daily to exercise your scalp.
>
> *Hands:* Washing your hands with soap is a major way to keep from spreading disease. Dry thoroughly after every washing. Hand washing is appropriate before meals, after visiting the bathroom, and at other times as needed. Trim your nails and clean under the nails. (Hint: If you do a lot of dirty work, scrape nails across a piece of soap before you start work. This makes cleanup easier.)
>
> *Feet:* Your feet support your body in its daily activities. They should be washed thoroughly every night, and each day should start with clean socks. Cut toenails straight across to prevent ingrown nails. Be sure that shoes fit well and are not too small or too large.
>
> *Teeth:* Brush and floss your teeth at least twice a day. Eat well-balanced meals and cut down on sweet snacks. Talk about the proper way to brush and floss.

- If you desire, talk about other habits that lead to good health. Use some of the following ideas or others of your own choosing: immunizations, using clean eating and drinking utensils, keeping flies away from yourself and your food, covering your mouth when sneezing, and so on.
- Have each child make a "personal health" poster by cutting out magazine pictures that remind them of the preceding activity. Glue the pictures to a small piece of poster board.
- Display these posters at a recognition night.

Personal Grooming

Materials Needed

Thank-you card, envelope, stamp, pen.

Before You Meet

Arrange for a beautician to come and visit with your group. Ask him or her to teach the children about proper care of hair, skin, and nails. (Avoid makeup instruction.)

Activity

- Have a presentation on good grooming.
- Follow up by having the children sign and mail a thank-you card to your guest speaker.

Family Ideas

Evaluate and organize family grooming supplies so everyone can readily find what he or she needs to stay well groomed.

A Healthy Food Banquet

Materials Needed

Pamphlets about good nutrition (available through your local health department), paper for word strips, a marker, plates, utensils, napkins.

Before You Meet

Prepare to teach your group about the basic food groups. Include instruction on what the food groups are and how many servings they need daily.

Assign each child to bring an item from one of the food groups to share with the other children. Specify which food group their item should come from.

Make word strips to identify each food group.

Activity

- Give a brief lesson on good nutrition and the basic food groups. Hand out a pamphlet for each child to take home.
- Arrange the food that the children brought on a table or counter. Give each person a pencil and paper. Instruct them to list each item and which food group it belongs to. Review the correct answers with them. Use the word strips to label the food.
- Have a banquet with the children. Remind them to choose something from each food group.

Family Ideas

Discuss nutritious snacks with your child. Choose one and prepare it as a family.

Making a Modest-Clothing Collage

Materials Needed

Heavy paper, scissors, glue.

Before You Meet

Gather catalogs and other magazines to cut collage pictures from. If you do not have enough, ask the Relief Society or a local department store for old copies. Make your own collage of pictures featuring modest clothing. Use this to show the children what they will be doing.

Activity

- Talk with the children about what it means to dress modestly. Briefly explain why it is important to dress modestly.
- Show the collage you made. Talk about how you put it together.
- Give the children the magazines and other materials and have them put together their own Modest-Clothing Collage.
- Have the children assist in cleanup. Encourage them to share their collages with their families.

Hospitality

*To help me learn how I can have good
relationships with others and how I
can help others be comfortable in groups.*

Table Settings

Materials Needed

Tablecloth, plates, glasses, silverware, cloth napkins, silk flowers, Styrofoam (egg cartons or bakery or meat trays work well), scissors, a clear goblet.

Before You Meet

Learn how to fold napkins several different ways.

Activity

- Teach the children how to set the table. Discuss the proper placement of plates, glasses, silverware, and napkins. Give everyone the chance to practice this.
- Practice pretty, creative ways to fold napkins.
- Let each child make a simple floating flower for a centerpiece. Cut a flat piece of Styrofoam to fit under a silk flower. Carefully push the stem of the flower through a small hole in the Styrofoam. Trim the stem to one inch and bend it to hold it to the Styrofoam. Show the children how this can become an easy centerpiece by filling a clear goblet with water and placing the flower in it. A couple of drops of food coloring can be added to the water if desired. Let them take home their own floating flowers. (For additional centerpiece ideas see "Making a Table Centerpiece," p. 48.)

Family Ideas

Use the good tableware for a special family dinner. Let your child use her centerpiece.

Making a Table Centerpiece

Materials Needed

A large rectangular lace paper doily (or fabric placemat) for each child, two or three colors of curling ribbon, several bright colors of paper, a ribbon shredder, a hole puncher, two small plastic bags for each child, a large silk flower, other seasonal items.

Before You Meet

Shred one yard of ribbon in each color and use the hole puncher to punch confetti from some of the colored paper.

Activity

- Demonstrate how to make this centerpiece by placing the lace paper doily in the center of a table. Arrange the shredded ribbon in the center of the doily and place the silk flower on top. Sprinkle the colored-paper confetti around the outside edges of the ribbon but on the lace paper doily.
- Demonstrate how the centerpiece can match the season by replacing the silk flower with another item. Use a pinecone, an Easter egg, a small gourd, a tree ornament, or other seasonal item.
- Show the children how this centerpiece can be used again by placing the shredded ribbon in one plastic bag and the colored-paper confetti in another. Roll the lace paper doily and loosely tie with string or a rubber band.
- Have the children shred their own ribbon and punch their own confetti. Store in plastic bags. Give each child a lace paper doily.
- Encourage them to use their new table centerpiece at home.

Family Ideas

Ask your child to use her table centerpiece for a special dinner.

Table Manners

Materials Needed

Necessary food for the menu you have selected, plates, glasses, utensils, napkins.

Before You Meet

Plan and prepare a luncheon for the children. You may desire to delegate some of the food assignments to them.
Set the table and have everything ready when they arrive.

Activity

- Briefly discuss with the children some basic table manners. Encourage their thoughts and ideas. Explain that this luncheon is for learning and practicing good table manners.
- Serve lunch. Take your time and let the children enjoy learning together.

Family Ideas

Discuss good table manners as a family. Determine one thing your family could improve in, and work on it together for a week.

Hosting a Party

Materials Needed

Refreshments, supplies for the games you have planned.

Before You Meet

Invite a Primary achievement group from another ward to come to a party.

Have a planning meeting with your children. Plan a "get to know you" activity, some games, and refreshments for the party. Make the necessary assignments. Discuss what it means to be a good host or hostess. Remind them that the objective is to make the other children feel welcome and to help them enjoy themselves. Explain that they will need to mingle with the other children, help them with the games, and serve the refreshments.

Activity

- Set up and prepare before the other ward arrives.
- Welcome the other children to the party and have a "get to know you" activity.
- Play games.
- Serve refreshments.
- Thank the guests for coming.
- Clean up.

Family Ideas

Discuss ways you can make people feel welcome and comfortable in your home. Invite someone special to have dinner with your family and practice these hospitality skills.

Hosting a Program

Materials Needed

Puppets, rhythm instruments, or other items necessary for the program part of this achievement activity (see "Rhythm Instruments and Fun Songs," p. 5, and "Making Puppets," p. 9), table decorations (see "Making a Table Centerpiece," p. 48).

Before You Meet

Make and distribute invitations for each child's parents. Also include an invitation to the bishopric member over the Primary.
Decide on a light refreshment.

Activity

- Set up tables for the parents to sit at. Place previously made table decorations on the tablecloth.
- As the parents arrive, have the children escort them to their tables.
- Have the children serve the refreshments to their parents.
- Allow time for the refreshments to be enjoyed.
- Begin the program. As an alternative, have the program before the refreshments.

Family Ideas

Write your child a note telling her about how you felt during the program.

Writing Thank-You Notes

Materials Needed

Cards, envelopes, stamps, pens.

Before You Meet

Assign the children to bring the name and address of someone they would like to thank for something special they have done. Encourage them to discuss this with their families to get ideas. Also have them each bring a postage stamp.

See "Making Greeting Cards" on p. 8 to precede this activity.

Activity

- Discuss the importance of thanking others. Point out that this can be done in person, on the phone, or by writing a short note.
- Teach them how to write a short note inside the card you give them to thank the person they have chosen.
- Teach them how to address and stamp the envelopes. Mail their cards at the local post office or place in a mailbox for pickup.

Family Ideas

Work together as a family to make a thank-you card and small treat for someone special.

Having a Recognition Meeting

Materials Needed

Awards certificates, refreshments.

Before You Meet

Schedule a time and place for your recognition meeting.
Meet with the children to plan the meeting. Include the following:

Opening song
Prayer (child)
Welcome (child)
Musical presentation (group)
Two testimonies (children)
Presentations of achievement days awards (leader)
Closing song
Prayer (child)
Refreshments (served by children)

Delegate some children to arrive early to help set up for the meeting, and the others to help clean up.

Activity

- Set up for the meeting.
- Have the recognition meeting as outlined.
- Clean up.

Family Ideas

Have a family recognition night. Recognize the efforts and accomplishments of each family member.

Outdoor Fun
and Skills

*To learn skills that will help me enjoy
the creations of our Father in Heaven.*

Outdoor Alphabet Game

Materials Needed

Paper and pencils, whistle, small treat.

Activity

- Divide the children into groups of two, or if the group is not large, allow them to participate individually.
- Have the children write the letters of the alphabet down the left side of the paper.
- Tell the children the rules of the game:

    1. Find one item in nature for every letter of the alphabet.
    2. An item can only be used once on your list.
    3. Do not go out of the designated area.
    4. Do not move an item. Leave nature the way it is.
    5. Sounds and smells are acceptable.
    6. When the children hear the whistle they must return immediately.

- At the end of fifteen minutes, blow the whistle. You can decide on a longer time if you wish.
- The winning group is the one that finds the most items. Have the members of this group pass out the treat to the other children.

Feeding Wild Birds

Materials Needed

Peanut butter, cornmeal, heavy twine, egg carton, wild birdseed, cup of gravel, hammer, nails.

Before You Meet

Gather enough pinecones for every child to have one. Locate a fence post and ask permission to use it for a bird feeder. Use a local college, university, or bird watchers club as a resource.

Activity

- Talk about wild birds in your area.
- Begin making the first bird feeder by cutting off and discarding the top of the egg carton and then punching a small drainage hole in the bottom of each egg cup.
- Go to the previously located fence post.
- Nail the egg carton to the top of the fence post.
- Fill four cups with gravel and the other eight with birdseed.
- Go back from time to time and check on it.
- Begin making the second bird feeder by giving every child a piece of twine and a pinecone.
- Tie the twine around the bottom of the pinecone. Allow several inches on the end for hanging from a tree.
- Mix equal portions of peanut butter and cornmeal—about two tablespoons per child.
- Spoon mixture into pinecone "petals."
- Have children take their pinecone feeders home to tie on a tree branch.

Family Ideas

Help your child find an easily seen branch to tie the pinecone feeder to.

Learning to Build a Campfire

Materials Needed

Bucket of water, rake, small shovel, tinder (tiny dry twigs, dry weed tops, dry shredded bark, etc.), kindling (small dry branches about as thick as your finger or thumb), fuel (larger dead branches).

Before You Meet

After determining a site for your campfire, obtain permission, if necessary, from local authorities. Have an exact location selected before you bring the children to their achievement day activity.

Activity

- Explain that a prepared fire site should always be used, if available. Explain that when a fire site is not available it is necessary to find the best place for a fire. Look for a bare spot, with a gravel or sandy base, that is well away from trees and bushes.
- Go to the area you have located and clear a circle about ten feet across. Rake away anything that can burn. Place the water at the edge of the fire site.
- Talk about safety rules that apply to campfires.
- Explain and show the three kinds of wood needed to build a fire.
- Begin the fire by laying tinder at the center of the fire site. Arrange the kindling so it will catch its flame from the tinder. After the kindling is burning, begin to lay fuel on the fire. Add enough fuel to make coals for your cooking project (see "Outdoor Cooking." p. 60).
- Everything you have learned is also applicable for prepared fire sites.
- When the cooking is over, show how to make sure the fire is completely out, and clean up.

Family Ideas

Ask your child to help you with a fire the next time the family has a campout.

Outdoor Cooking

Materials Needed

Materials are dependent upon the items you choose to cook.

Before You Meet

First time outdoor cooking should be kept simple. Choose recipes with that in mind.

Activity

- After the campfire has been made and has burned down to coals, begin the cooking achievement.
- Choose from the following outdoor recipes or use a recipe of your own.

    Tinfoil dinner: Shape hamburger into a patty. Thinly slice or grate a small potato and carrot. Place onto heavy-duty aluminum foil (or two layers of regular strength foil) and season with salt and pepper. Fold the foil into a tight package. Cook on the coals for about fifteen to twenty minutes.
    Corn on the cob roast: Open the corn's husk and remove the threadlike silk (do not remove husk). Wash and close the husk over the corn. Dip the corn in water and lay on the coals. Roast about seven to ten minutes, turning often.
    Biscuit on a stick: Shape biscuit dough around the outside of a clean stick. Toast it over the coals until it is lightly brown on the outside and done on the inside. Serve with honey butter or jam.
    Baked Apple: Cut out the core from a raw apple and replace with a small pat of butter, some cinnamon, and a little brown sugar. Wrap the apple in aluminum foil and bake for twenty-five to thirty minutes.
    S'mores: Toast a marshmallow over the coals until lightly brown. Place it between two chocolate-covered shortbread cookies.

- If you desire, invite parents to this cookout.

Preparing for a Hike

Before You Meet

Assign each child to bring items for a small hiking kit: a small whistle, a large plastic garbage sack, two adhesive bandages, a large handkerchief or bandanna, and a large safety pin.

If you are making trail mix, see "Making a Hiker's Snack" in "Outdoor Fun and Skills," p. 63.

Activity

- Discuss how to prepare for going on a hike. Include a discussion of proper dress (especially shoes), the buddy system, what to do if you become separated from the group, having a destination, taking water, and so on.
- Talk about the use of each item in the hiking kit (whistle for use if lost, garbage sack to make an emergency rain poncho, bandanna for head scarf or large bandage, etc.)
- Have the children lay out their bandannas, and, except for the safety pin, arrange the items on top. Fold the bandanna over the items and close securely with the safety pin. This should be folded small enough to fit in a pocket or fanny pack.
- Make trail mix at this point, if you have chosen to do so.
- Talk about a future hike: where you are going, what the children need to bring, and so on.

Going on a Hike

Before You Meet

Decide on where you are hiking. If there is someone who can tell the children about plants and animals you might see, invite him or her to be a guide.

Contact each of the children and have them bring their hiking kit (see "Preparing for a Hike," p. 61) and a canteen or other water container. Remind them of other preparations as necessary.

Provide for adequate transportation, if necessary. Fill out any travel permits required by your ward or stake.

Activity

- Gather the children and assign each child a partner.
- Talk about the purpose of telling someone where you are going and when you will be back. Help the children understand that you have done that.
- Go on your hike.
- When you return, briefly talk about what you have seen.

Making a Hiker's Snack

Materials Needed

Peanuts, sugar-coated cereal, dried fruit, candy-coated chocolate pieces, reclosable plastic bags.

Activity

- Have each child measure a quarter cup each of peanuts, sugar-coated cereal, and dried fruit into the plastic bag.
- Add one large handful of candy-coated chocolate pieces.
- Reclose the bag and shake it until thoroughly mixed.
- Store in a cool place until used for a hike.

Personal Preparedness

*To develop personal habits and skills
that will help me provide for myself.*

Visiting a Bank

Materials Needed

One penny for each child, thank-you card, envelope, stamp, pen.

Before You Meet

Call a local bank to schedule a group visit. Request that someone conduct a tour and teach the children the difference between a savings account, a checking account, and a loan.

Provide for adequate transportation, if necessary. Fill out any tour permits required by your ward or stake.

Activity

- Tour the bank.
- Explain to the children that they should use wisdom in planning what they will do with each and every cent they get. They can save it or spend it. Give a penny to each child and challenge them to begin that very day.
- Have the children sign and mail a thank-you card to the individual who gave you the tour.

Family Ideas

Help your child set up a personal savings fund.

Growing Sprouts

Materials Needed

Window screen material, alfalfa seeds, prepared alfalfa sprouts.

Before You Meet

Ask each child to bring a quart-size canning jar and ring. Prepare a salad or sandwiches using some alfalfa sprouts.

Prepare the following sprouting instruction sheet for each child.

1. Measure one tablespoon of alfalfa seeds into a quart jar, fill one-third full of water, and soak for twelve hours.
2. Drain and lay the jar on its side.
3. Rinse with cool water and drain (two to three times each day).
4. Continue step 3 for three to five days until the sprouts have matured.

Activity

-   Serve the prepared refreshment.
-   Explain what sprouts are. Demonstrate the instruction steps for sprouting.
-   Have the children trace around the bottle openings onto the screen. Cut out each round piece of screen and fit each piece into a jar ring.
-   Let each child measure one tablespoon of alfalfa seeds into her jar. Give each an instruction sheet. Encourage them to try making their own sprouts at home.

Family Ideas

Grow different types of sprouts and substitute them for lettuce occasionally.

Learning About Communication

Materials Needed

Check selected communication activities for necessary materials.

Before You Meet

Set up each area you will be using. If you desire, involve other adults in setting up and monitoring the communication areas.

Activity

- Briefly discuss what it means to communicate. Ask the children to name some of the many ways people communicate.
- Have the group of children play each selected game or activity. Have them name the kind of communication they experienced as they finish each area. Select two or more communication activities or use some of your own.

  Non-verbal communication: Place the names of several animals on slips of paper and have each child choose one of the slips. Ask each child to act out the animal without using any sounds or words.

  Foreign language: Have someone come and speak to the children in a foreign language. Talk briefly about how communication takes place in every language. Teach one or two simple phrases in a foreign language.

  Body language: Write several emotions on individual slips of paper and have the children choose one apiece. Have each act out her chosen emotion without making any sound.

  Sign language: Ask someone to come and talk about how hearing-impaired individuals "speak" to others. Teach the alphabet and a few simple words or phrases in sign language.

  Written communication: Divide the children into pairs and give each pair several small pieces of paper. Tell the children that one person is to find out about the other person (birth date, favorite color, special experience, etc.), but the other person can only write the answers to the questions instead of saying them out loud. After a specified length of time, switch roles. If time permits, have the children tell what they learned about each other.

  Written codes: Explain that some communication is done in written code. Ask the children if they have ever used a written code. Some codes might use numbers or symbols for letters. Have a simple sentence written on pieces of paper for the children to decipher. Have the code translation available for the children to use.

- Gather the children and ask them what they learned about communication.

Family Ideas

Follow up with a family home evening on communication and ask your child to tell what she learned from the achievement day.

Cooperation Games

Materials Needed

A watch with a second hand, simple refreshments, any materials necessary for selected games listed below.

Before You Meet

Set up each area you are using. If you desire, involve other adults in doing this and monitoring the different activities.

Activity

- Explain what cooperation is and briefly discuss how it helps us in almost everything we do. Help the children understand that cooperation is more than doing things together, it is also helping one another do tasks better in a positive way.
- Have the group of children play each selected game. Time each attempt and encourage them to try again for faster time. Select two or more of the sample games or use some of your own.

  Relay cooperation: Have the children line up. Give the first child a ball and have her pass it over her head to the next child. The second child will pass the ball between her legs to the third child. Repeat this relay pattern until the ball has gone to the end of the line and back to the beginning.

  Blind obstacle: Blindfold all children except one. Have all the blindfolded children line up behind the "leader" child and place their hands on the shoulders of the child in front of them. The leader must now lead the line of blindfolded children through a simple obstacle course. Repeat until every child has the chance to be the leader.

  Bean pick-up: Place a large handful of beans in the center of a table. Give each child two toothpicks. When they are told to start, every child must pick up a bean with their toothpicks and place it in a bowl or shallow container. Repeat until all the beans are in the bowl.

  2' x 6' squeeze: Put a 2' x 6' board on the floor. Ask the children to line up on the board. The first person in line must walk around the rest of the people but everyone must stay on the board. If anyone gets knocked off the board, the penalty is three seconds added to her time. Repeat until every child has had the opportunity to "squeeze" down the line.

Memory observation: Place twenty items on a large tray and cover with a cloth. Place the tray in front of the children and remove the cloth for about one minute. Cover the tray and have the children tell you what was on the tray. This is a group effort achievement and does not need to be timed.

Clothesline relay: Have a rope (clothesline) with four clothespins on it about ten feet from the starting line. This clothesline can be held apart by two chairs or other similar items. Place a small basket containing a shirt and two socks in front of the line of children. Have the first child take the clothes basket to the rope and pin the clothes to the line. That child then runs back and tags the second child. The second child must run to the clothesline, take the clothes off, put them in the basket, and take the basket back to the starting line. Repeat until every child has the opportunity to play this relay.

- When all of the cooperation games have been done, celebrate with a small refreshment.

Family Ideas

Talk with your child about what cooperation is, what she learned about it, and how your family uses it in daily living.

Bike Tire Repair

Materials Needed

Flat-tire repair kit with enough supplies for your group, a tub of water (to help locate the leak), an air pump, other tools as specified by the parent.

Before You Meet

Arrange for a parent to come and teach the children how to repair a flat tire on a bicycle. He may need you to arrange for an assistant for him, depending on the size of your group.

Contact parents to explain that the children will have a hands-on experience for bicycle tire repair. Ask the children to bring a bicycle (theirs or a family member's) that needs a flat repaired. If parents feel a new tube is needed, they should send it with their child.

Activity

- Have the demonstration on flat-tire repair.
- Let the children repair their own tires. Assist as needed.

Family Ideas

Fix and repair all the family bikes and go for a bike ride together.

This activity works well in the spring, when many tires are flat and in need of repair.

Safety and Emergency Preparedness

To learn how to be safe and what to do in emergencies.

Basic First Aid

Materials Needed

A display of basic first-aid supplies.

Before You Meet

Be prepared to teach basic first-aid techniques.

Write the following terms on slips of paper: *minor cut, minor burn, blister, insect bite,* and *nosebleed.* Place the papers in a bag.

Activity

- Demonstrate proper first-aid care for the following: cuts and scratches, minor burns, blisters on hands or feet, insect bites, and nosebleeds.
- Let the children take turns drawing the slips of paper out of the bag. Have them review with the group how you would treat that wound.

Family Ideas

Make or update a family first-aid kit.

Making a Personal Emergency Kit

Materials Needed

For each child: triangular bandage (use an old cotton scarf or other cotton material), three adhesive bandages, two large safety pins, a Popsicle stick or tongue depressor with twelve inches of adhesive tape wrapped around it, alcohol wipe, small tissue pack, one-inch square of cardboard with one yard of thread wrapped around it, sewing needle, small package of gum or hard candy, reclosable plastic bag, other items if necessary for your area.

Activity

- Fold the triangular bandage and pin with safety pins.
- Place sewing needle securely into the wrapped thread.
- Talk about each item and how it can be used in an emergency.
- Place all kit items into the plastic bag. Close securely.

Family Ideas

Be aware of what is in the personal emergency kit and help your child keep it current.

Bike Safety

Materials Needed

Bikes for each child, equipment to make an obstacle course.

Before You Meet

Ask each child to bring a bike. Be prepared to teach the children bicycle safety rules. Contact your local police to obtain bike safety handouts with a copy of safety rules.

Arrange for the use of a playground or parking lot for bike riding. Set up a simple bike obstacle course.

Activity

- Discuss safety rules for riding bikes.
- Take turns riding through the obstacle course; stress safety.

Family Ideas

Ask your child to review the bike safety rules with you.

Finding Household Hazards

Before You Meet

Prepare a room (preferably one you will not be meeting in) with several obvious household hazards such as a skate in the middle of the floor, matches within easy reach, etc.

Copy a "Home Safety Checklist" (or any other safety list) for each child (see p. 79).

Activity

- Gather the children and ask what the word *safe* means to each of them. When they are done, ask what a safe house would be.
- Go over the "Home Safety Checklist" with the children and discuss how doing these things will keep your home safe.
- Have the children go to the room you prepared for them and find the household hazards.
- After all the hazards have been found, ask the children to tell you what must be done to correct them, and then make sure they are corrected.
- Have the children take their checklist home and check for safety hazards.

Family Ideas

Talk with your child about what she learned. Use her "Home Safety Checklist" in your home. Correct any hazards you find.

Home Safety Checklist

____ Stairways and halls kept free from boxes, toys, mops, brooms, tools, or other tripping hazards.

____ Stairways provided with a strong handrail.

____ Matches or lighters kept where children cannot get them.

____ Knives and other sharp instruments kept in a drawer out of reach of children.

____ Disinfectants, cleaning products, and poisons clearly marked and kept out of reach of children.

____ All medicines out of reach of children.

____ Furniture placed to allow clear passage.

____ Stoves located away from curtains.

____ Yard and play space free from holes, stones, broken glass, and other litter.

____ Cords kept from under rug.

____ Electric cords kept in good repair.

____ Emergency numbers and home address posted by each telephone.

____ Smoke detectors in place and checked regularly.

____ Fire extinguishers readily available.

_____

This is a basic list only. For a more complete list, contact a local safety organization such as a fire station, police department, or the Red Cross.

Visiting a Fire Station

Materials Needed

Thank-you card, envelope, stamp, pen.

Before You Meet

Contact your local fire station and schedule a brief tour. Request instruction on preventing fires in your home and what to do in case of a fire.

Provide for adequate transportation, if necessary. Fill out any travel permits required by your ward or stake.

Activity

- Have a tour of the fire station.
- Discuss fire prevention and safety.
- Conclude the activity by having children sign and mail a thank-you note to your guide.

Family Ideas

Plan a fire escape route from your home. Have a family fire drill.

Service
and Citizenship

*To help me enjoy serving others in my
family, my neighborhood, my ward,
and my country.*

Service Scavenger Hunt

Materials Needed

A printed list of chores for each group, a pencil, refreshments.

Before You Meet

Prepare a list of chores for your scavenger hunt, such as: sweep a sidewalk, vacuum a room, carry out garbage, read a child a story, and so on. Arrange for one adult to be with each group of children.

Activity

- Divide the children into two or more groups. Assign an adult to go with each group.
- Explain that you will give each group a list of service items you can do in your neighborhood. They are to go from home to home and ask if they can do one of the chores. The challenge is to see if each group can get their entire list completed.
- Pass out lists and begin the scavenger hunt.
- Meet back at a designated time and serve refreshments. Encourage the children to share their experiences.

Family Ideas

Make service a game! Draw family names and do secret services for that person all week.

Nursing Home Service Program

Materials Needed

Puppets, rhythm instruments, or other items necessary for this program.

Before You Meet

Contact the program director of a local nursing home and schedule this project. Check on a suggested program length. The suggested program in this achievement should be about fifteen to twenty minutes long. If you desire, ask about the possibility of playing a party game with the residents.

Decide what kind of program you will put on. This would be a great opportunity to use the puppet and rhythm instrument achievements. (See Rhythm Instruments and Fun Songs, p. 5, and Making Puppets, p. 9.)

Provide for adequate transportation, if necessary. Fill out any travel permits required by your ward or stake.

Activity

- Talk with the children about differences they may notice between nursing home programs and other programs. Discuss any concerns they may have.
- Set up the puppet theater.
- Have one of the children introduce the program.
- Use your rhythm instruments to present a song.
- Present a puppet play.
- Sing a fun song.
- Close the program by thanking the audience.
- Take down the puppet theater.
- If approved, play an appropriate party game with the residents.

Family Ideas

Support your child by attending this performance. Help her see the residents as children of Heavenly Father. With permission, select a resident to visit often as a family.

Preparing a Service Dinner

Materials Needed

Necessary ingredients to prepare your planned menu, supplies for the children to make a card to deliver with the meal.

Before You Meet

Contact your Relief Society president to determine a family or individual that may need a meal. Schedule a date and time for the meal to be brought to the family or individual.

Plan a simple menu that the children could help prepare.

Activity

- Discuss your menu with the children and delegate assignments for meal preparation.
- Prepare the meal and help the children as needed.
- Assign some of the children to make a greeting card for the family. Have all the children sign the card.
- Deliver the meal.

Family Ideas

Challenge the family to offer one act of secret service to someone in need.

Helping in the Nursery

Materials Needed

Refreshments, supplies for the art activity.

Before You Meet

Make arrangements with the Relief Society for your group to baby-sit in the nursery during homemaking meeting. Have a planning meeting with your group to prepare a simple art activity, a story, games, and a snack. Make assignments to individual children as needed. You may want to preface this activity with the "Baby-Sitting Workshop" on p. 36.

Activity

- Meet to set up before the nursery children arrive.
- Have a simple art activity.
- Serve refreshments.
- Read a short story.
- Play games as time permits.
- Clean up.

Family Ideas

Offer to baby-sit for a young family while they go to the temple or a church activity. Use the ideas the children learned from helping in the nursery.

Making a Talking Book

Materials Needed

A tape recorder and one cassette tape for every two children (put one book on each side), labels for cassettes.

Before You Meet

Contact parents and explain that the children will be making "talking books" to donate to a children's hospital, homeless shelter, or other organization of your choice. Request that the children bring a children's book to donate. Ask parents to make sure the book is on their child's reading level.

Activity

- Let the children practice reading their books once.
- Take turns recording the children reading their books. Have the children say, "Please turn the page," at the end of each page.
- Label the titles of the books onto each tape.
- Let children write who the book was donated by in the front of each book.
- Package books and tapes to be delivered at a later date.

Family Ideas

Make talking books to give to friends or family for Christmas or birthday gifts.

Preparing a Missionary Package

Materials Needed

A box, a missionary's address, paperback copies of the Book of Mormon, pictures of each child, pens, rubber cement, materials to make a greeting card for the missionary, a treat to send.

Before You Meet

Notify the parents to explain that the children need to earn enough money to buy a paperback Book of Mormon to send to a missionary. The children will also need to bring a small personal picture to glue on the inside cover of the book. Restrictions may apply to missionaries in some foreign countries.

Activity

- Assist each child in writing her personal testimony in the front of the Book of Mormon.
- Affix pictures in the books.
- Work as a group to make a greeting card for the missionary; make sure everyone signs it.
- Package the books, card, and treat for mailing.

Family Ideas

Write a family letter to a missionary of your choice.

Preparing a Flag Ceremony

Materials Needed

A flag.

Before You Meet

Gather interesting information about your country's flag.* Use an encyclopedia, a Scout handbook, or a local veterans organization as a resource. Make arrangements to present your flag ceremony at a local function (ward or community).

Activity

- Start the activity by telling the children that you are going to give them clues and you want them to guess what you are talking about. For instance, "This item must be treated with respect because it represents many people," "This item is sometimes called 'Old Glory,'" "This item is made from cloth," "If you hang this item upside down it indicates an emergency," "This item has thirteen stripes and fifty stars," etc.
- Discuss what the stripes, stars, and colors stand for and explain that a country's flag represents its people.
- Help the children understand basic rules about handling a flag. If possible, use a real flag. This information might include care, proper use, folding, etc.
- Plan and practice a flag ceremony. For flag ceremony ideas, see the following activity.

_____

For the sake of space, examples for this activity are based on the flag of the United States of America.

Flag Ceremony Ideas

A flag ceremony can be any ceremony where the flag is given proper acknowledgement and the Pledge of Allegiance is recited. The most common flag ceremony involves four to five individuals and is similar to the following one:

The spokesman is positioned at the podium, microphone, or other assigned place. The flag carrier(s) and two color guards are generally stationed at the back of the room.

Spokesman: Color guard, attention. Will the audience please rise. Color guard, present the colors. Will the audience please give the proper salute.

The flag carrier and color guard then advance to the flag stand, usually from the back of the room; the color guard is slightly behind and to each side of the flag carrier. If more than one flag is used, the national flag is held slightly higher than any other flag. The color guard always follows the flag(s).

Spokesman: Color guard, post the colors.

The flag carrier then places the flag into the flag stand and steps back into line with the color guard. The entire color guard salutes the flag.

Spokesman: Will the audience please repeat the Pledge of Allegiance with me.

The spokesman then faces the flag, salutes, and clearly speaks the Pledge of Allegiance with the audience.

Spokesman: Two. [The entire color guard discontinues the salute.] Color guard dismissed. The audience may be seated.

The spokesman then leaves the podium area.

Other ideas for a flag ceremony can be obtained from Scout handbooks, veterans organizations, or military public relations offices.

Touring Local Historic Sites

Materials Needed

Brochures of interesting sites (if available).

Before You Meet

Learn about your community's historical landmarks. Plan a short tour of a few area highlights.

Provide for adequate transportation, if necessary. Fill out any travel permits required by your ward or stake.

Activity

- Tour the planned historical sites. Discuss each one, asking the children how it influenced the growth and development of the community.

Family Ideas

Ask your child to share what she learned about the history of your community.

Spirituality

*To give me opportunities to learn the
gospel, share it with others,
and prepare for temple blessings.*

Using the Scriptures

Materials Needed

A bowl of small candy such as jelly beans.

Before You Meet

Ask the children to bring their scriptures to the activity. Make a list of scripture references for children to find during a scripture chase. You may want to use verses related to a central topic such as love, service, honesty, and so on. Use references from the Old Testament, New Testament, Book of Mormon, Doctrine and Covenants, and Pearl of Great Price.

Activity

- Familiarize the children with the scriptures by showing them where the Old Testament, New Testament, Book of Mormon, Doctrine and Covenants, and Pearl of Great Price are located in the scriptures. Give them a brief explanation of each of these sets of scriptures. Teach them how to look up different books in the scriptures using the list of the book names located in front of the Bible and Book of Mormon.
- Have a scripture chase. For example, begin by saying, "This verse is found in the New Testament. Matthew 25:21." As each child finds the verse, he or she may take a candy from the bowl. After they all have located the verse, select one child to read it to the group.

Family Ideas

Make a family game. Write the title of favorite scripture stories on index cards (Daniel in the Lions' Den, Jesus Healing the Ten Lepers, The Two Thousand Stripling Warriors, and so on). Divide into two teams. One team draws a card and acts out that title. The other team must guess the story and which set of scriptures it is found in (Old Testament, New Testament, Book of Mormon, Doctrine and Covenants, or Pearl of Great Price).

Preparing a Flannel Board Scripture Story

Materials Needed

Heavy interfacing material, fine-point permanent marker (black), crayons, scrap paper, iron, ironing board.

Before You Meet

Ask the children to decide on a scripture story they would like to tell their families, study the story, and decide what figures will be needed to tell the story.

Activity

- Give each child a piece of interfacing to draw the figures on. This may be done by direct drawing or by tracing from a pattern. Remind them to keep their flannel board ideas as simple as possible. (Use flannel board packets and the scripture readers available through the Church Distribution Center as resources for ideas.)
- After the figures, animals, or scenery have been drawn, add color by using the crayons.
- Cut out the flannel board figures.
- Seal the colors in place by placing a piece of scrap paper over the colored interfacing and pressing with a hot iron. Be sure that the paper covers the colored part completely or the crayon wax will get on the iron.
- Have the children assist with the cleanup.
- If time permits, have the children share their scripture stories with each other.

Family Ideas

Ask your child to share the flannel board story during family home evening or another appropriate time.

Making Scripture Bookmarks

Materials Needed

Heavy paper, scissors, hole punch, markers, yarn, clear contact paper (optional).

Before You Meet

Ask the children to bring their scriptures to the activity. Cut the paper to an appropriate size for bookmarks.

Activity

- Instruct the children to select one of their favorite verses from the scriptures. Give them plenty of time. Help them as needed. Talk to them about their favorite scripture stories and look up references of a special topic. Exploring the scriptures with them is an important part of this activity.
- Have them copy their favorite verse onto the precut paper with markers. Have extra paper available in case they make a mistake. Let them decorate the opposite side as desired.
- (Optional) Place the bookmark between two pieces of clear contact paper and seal. Trim around the edges.
- Use the hole punch to punch a hole at the top of each bookmark.
- Teach them how to thread several lengths of yarn through the hole to make a tassel.

Family Ideas

Challenge each family member to memorize his or her favorite scripture verse and to be able to recite it at the next family home evening.

Building Temple Memories

Materials Needed

Camera with color film, small picture of local temple for each child, stationery and matching envelopes, pens, scrapbook paper.

Before You Meet

Contact the children and ask them to come in "Sunday best" attire for this achievement activity.

Activity

- Take the children to the local temple grounds. Remind them that this is a reverent place to be.
- Quietly discuss the beauty and peace of the temple grounds.
- Take a picture of each child. If you wish, allow each child to choose where to have her picture taken.
- Give each child an envelope, stationery, and pen. Ask them to write about how being close to the temple makes them feel. Have them place the note into the envelope but leave it unsealed.
- Collect the notes from the children.
- Develop the pictures.
- Mount each child's picture, unsealed envelope (flap side out), and the temple picture on a scrapbook page. At an appropriate time, give the pages to the children.

Family Ideas

Share your feelings about the temple with your child before she goes on this achievement day activity.

Making Temple Handkerchiefs

Materials Needed

A small, plain white handkerchief for each child, gathered lace, white thread, straight pins, scissors, two sewing machines, acid-free envelopes (found in most large copy centers).

Before You Meet

Depending on the size of your group, you may need to arrange for an additional assistant.

Activity

- Each child should pin lace around the edges of the handkerchief, making small tucks at the corners so lace will lay flat.
- Stitch the lace on the handkerchief by using a zigzag stitch.
- Carefully fold the handkerchief and store it in an acid-free envelope to prevent fabric from yellowing.

Family Ideas

Plan a family trip to the temple visitors' center.

Making Sacrament Bread

Materials Needed

Ingredients and equipment to make bread, refreshments.

Before You Meet

Approve this activity with the bishop. Be sure to schedule which Sunday the sacrament bread will be brought.

Select a basic white bread recipe. Collect necessary ingredients.

Read the story of the Last Supper (Luke 22:7–20). Be prepared to tell it in your own words. Emphasize that Jesus knew he would soon leave his disciples, and he wanted them to continue to remember him and his teachings. For this reason he gave them the sacrament. This is why we partake of the sacrament too.

Activity

- Tell the story of the Last Supper.
- Share your testimony of the importance of the sacrament and the special opportunity to make the sacrament bread. Encourage an attitude of reverence.
- Prepare bread, giving each child a chance to measure and add ingredients, knead the dough, and shape the loaves.
- Play quiet games and have a refreshment while the dough rises and bakes. If time does not permit this, you may conclude the activity and finish baking the bread yourself.

Family Ideas

Discuss things your family can do during the sacrament to be more reverent and to help you think more of the Savior at this special time.

Sports and
Physical Fitness

*To help me learn how to keep my body
strong through physical activities.*

Learning About Fitness

Before You Meet

Invite someone with a background in fitness to come and speak with the children about the importance of a healthy diet and exercise. Be specific about the amount of time you need him or her to take. Ask your guest to assist you in the exercise portion of this achievement.

Activity

- Introduce your guest and give him or her any needed time to talk about eating well and proper exercise.
- Talk about how strengthening and stretching exercises help us, and do some of the following or use some of your own choosing.

  Paper crumple: Take a piece of paper in one hand and crumple it up until it has become a tight little ball. Repeat with other hand or do both hands together.

  Body pull-in: Begin by lying flat on your back. Slowly pull your legs up until your knees touch your chin. Count to five and slowly return to starting position. Repeat.

  Body stretch: Lie on your stomach. Raise your arms, chest, and legs until only your abdomen is touching the ground. Stretch your arms and legs out to the side. Count to five. Return to the starting position. Repeat.

  Toe touch: Stand with your feet about a foot apart and arms extended out to the side. Bend sideways and touch your foot with the opposite hand. Repeat with other hand and foot.

  Leg stretch: Place a 2' x 4' board on the ground. Stand on the board. Slowly move backward until only the front third of your foot is left on the board. Allow back part of foot to relax and hang over the edge. You may need to stretch your arms out for balance. Count to fifteen. Step back on the board. Repeat.

Family Ideas

Have your child share the stretching and strengthening exercises with the family. Make them a part of a daily exercise program.

Playing Outdoor Games

Materials Needed

Items needed to play the games.

Before You Meet

Assign each child to teach the group how to play her favorite outdoor game. Follow up with the children to find out if they need any special equipment such as balls and so on. Also, make sure that two children don't prepare the same game.

Activity

- Let each of the children have a turn teaching the group their favorite outdoor game. Repeat the games and play as long as time permits.

Family Ideas

As a family, play one of the games that your child learned at the activity.

Indoor Golf

Materials Needed

Nine cardboard boxes, marker, perforated plastic golf balls or Ping-Pong balls.

Before You Meet

Mark each of the nine boxes with a number, one through nine. Prepare the golf course by placing boxes around the game area.

Activity

- Give each child a golf ball.
- One at a time, have the children throw the ball toward the first "hole." If it does not go in, try again from where the ball landed.
- Continue until all nine holes have been done.
- If you wish, keep score.

Family Ideas

Borrow the "course" or make your own and play for a family home evening activity.

This game can also be played outdoors.

Outdoor Olympics

Materials Needed

Various items to make an obstacle course, tape measure, stopwatch, paper, safety pins, ribbon, gold candy pieces, Frisbee, tennis ball.

Before You Meet

Make name tags for each child, using the name of a country instead of personal names.

Make gold medals for each child, using ribbon and a gold candy piece.

Make an obstacle course for the children to run through, using tires, tricycles, and so on.

Activity

- Let each of the children draw a name tag out of a bag. Pin it on them. This will be the country they will represent.
- Proceed with the following events. Let each of the children have at least two turns at each event. The emphasis will be on bettering their own performance. You may want to give them some practice time for each event.

    1. Frisbee throw: Measure the distance the Frisbee is thrown.
    2. Fifty-yard dash: Time each child individually.
    3. Tennis ball throw: Measure the distance the ball is thrown.
    4. Running broad jump: Measure the distance jumped.
    5. Obstacle course: Time each child.
    6. Standing broad jump: Measure the distance jumped.

- Have a closing ceremony. Present each of the children with a gold medal for their efforts.

Family Ideas

Have a family fun night making an obstacle course in your backyard.

Indoor Track and Field Relay

Materials Needed

Soccer ball, four ground markers, Frisbee or paper plate, basketball, cardboard box, 2' x 4' board, masking tape, long piece of butcher paper, marker or crayon, watch with a second hand (optional).

Before You Meet

Lay out the obstacle course as explained in the activity instructions. You may desire to involve parents or other adults in running and timing the course.

Activity

- Divide the children into two groups. Place one group at the beginning of the course and the second group at the end. This is a group relay course.
- As a child from group one finishes the course from beginning to end, she will tag a child from group two. The child from group two finishes the course from end to beginning and then will tag a child from group one. Repeat until everyone has a chance at the course.
- Use the following sections or some of your own choosing.

  Balance beam: The 2' x 4' board is laid flat on the ground. Walk along the board from one end to the other. Anyone falling off the board must start over.
  Discus throw: Make two masking tape lines about ten feet apart. Stand at one line and carefully toss the Frisbee or paper plate onto or over the other line.
  Standing long jump: Make two masking tape lines four feet apart. Jump from one line to the other.
  Soccer: Place floor markers about two feet apart in a straight line. Have a beginning line and a finish line marked two feet from the first and last floor markers. Using only your feet, weave the soccer ball in and out of the markers and over the finish line.
  High jump: Tape butcher paper to the wall. Make a mark as high as you can reach. Holding the marker, jump as high as you can and make another mark on the paper at the height of your jump.
  Basketball: Use a basketball standard (if available) or a cardboard box. Mark a throw line. Stand at the throw line and throw the basketball through the hoop (or into the box). Five tries only.
  Fifteen-foot dash: Mark off fifteen feet. Holding one foot, hop to the finish line. This should be the last section.

Folk Dancing

Materials Needed

Tapes or records of folk music, tape recorder or record player.

Before You Meet

If you do not feel comfortable with this achievement day activity, invite someone to assist you. You can also use square dancing or do this as a father-daughter activity.

Activity

- Teach the basic steps for the dance.
- Rehearse several times until everyone feels more comfortable with the steps.
- Dance to the music.
- Depending on time, learn one or two dances.

Achievement Day Calendar

For the Month of _____

Date _____ Time _____ Place _____

- Achievement area and purpose

  _____

  _____

- Special needs or items to bring

  _____

  _____

- Family ideas

  _____

  _____

Date _____ Time _____ Place _____

- Achievement area and purpose

  _____

  _____

- Special needs or items to bring

  _____

  _____

- Family ideas

  _____

  _____

Achievement Day Calendar

For the Month of _July_

Date _12_ Time _9:00 a.m._ Place _the ward_

- Achievement area and purpose

  outdoor fun & skills
  build a bird feeder & learn an outdoor game

- Special needs or items to bring

  will have all material you need

- Family ideas

  Help your child find a place to hang
  their bird feeder.

Date _26_ Time _5:30 p.m._ Place _Jefferson Park_

- Achievement area and purpose

  outdoor fun & skills
  building a campfire, having a cookout

- Special needs or items to bring

  bring parents

- Family ideas

  Your child is learning to build a campfire.
  Have them help you next time you go
  Camping.

Presented to

_____

for completing achievements

in the area of:

_____

_____   _____
Achievement Day Leader   *Primary President*

Recognition Certificate

Presented to _____

for completing achievements

in the area of:

_____

Achievement Day Leader

Primary President

Recognition Certificate

Awarded to

for completing achievements in the area of

Achievement Day Leader

Primary President